MOZART

14 OF HIS EASIEST PIECES FOR THE PIANO

A PRACTICAL PERFORMING EDITION

Mozart at 11
Oil painting by T. Helbling
(Stiftung Mozarteum, Salzburg)

Contents

Selections are placed in approximate order of difficulty.

Alfred

Second Edition

Cover art: A detail from Vienna Seen from the Rotenturm-Gate *(circa 1740)*
by Johann Adam Delsenbach
Oil on canvas
Erich Lessing/Art Resource, New York

WOLFGANG AMADEUS MOZART

His first efforts at composition began when he was only four years old. By the time he was six he had composed dozens of remarkable pieces for the keyboard as well as for other instruments, and was performing for emperors and empresses in the courts of Europe. At eight he startled the King of England by playing at sight every difficult piece of music put before him, and by improvising during public concerts. At the age of ten he wrote an oratorio, and at eleven he wrote his first opera. At thirteen he was appointed Chapel Master at the court of the Archbishop of Salzburg. At fourteen he received an advanced degree in music from the Royal Academy in Mantua, Italy, and was knighted by the Pope. By this time he had successful operas running for weeks of performance at La Scala, the great opera house in Milan, Italy, and was no longer regarded as a child prodigy, but fully recognized as a great master.

His name was Wolfgang Amadeus Mozart, and he was born in Salzburg, Austria, on January 27, 1756.

Wolfgang's father, Leopold Mozart, was a famous violinist who held an important position as the assistant conductor of the orchestra of the Archbishop of Salzburg. He was a brilliant musician and an outstanding teacher, and he was quick to recognize the unusual talents of his two remarkable children. Wolfgang's sister, Anna Maria (Nannerl), was almost as gifted as her brother. Leopold virtually gave up his post with the court orchestra to devote his time to developing the talents of his two children, and to arranging concert appearances for them.

During his extensive travels, the young Wolfgang was quick to assimilate the best of what he heard from the greatest musicians he encountered. In London he studied composition with Johann Christian Bach, a son of the great Johann Sebastian Bach. In Germany he was impressed and influenced by the musical discipline of the famous Mannheim Orchestra, with its remarkable dynamic contrasts, ranging from the softest *pianissimo* to the loudest *fortissimo*. In Bologna, Italy, he was heard by the great Padre Martini, who became his mentor and instructor and helped him to prepare for his degree.

When he was 26 years old, Mozart married Constanze von Weber, over his father's objections. The course of his married life never ran smooth. Although his career was artistically successful, he was a poor business man, and had a difficult time managing his affairs, especially after his father was no longer able to travel with him. Although his music was performed all over Europe, even by amateurs and (to Mozart's delight) by street musicians, Mozart died in poor circumstances. Believing that he had been poisoned, perhaps by a jealous musician, he died on December 5, 1791, and was buried in an unmarked grave.

Mozart's works contain the essence as well as the most perfect of those compositions which are correctly called *classical*. His fame came first as a composer and performer of music for the harpsichord, but the piano began to be perfected, and by the time he was 21, he had selected it for his main instrument. He became the first of the great composers for piano.

Of Wolfgang Amadeus Mozart, Haydn said, "He is the greatest composer I know, personally or by reputation. He has taste, and furthermore he has the greatest possible knowledge of composition."

Mozart would never bow to the common practice of allowing royalty to dictate how music should be composed. When the Emperor heard his opera *The Abduction from the Seraglio*, he said, "It is too beautiful, my dear Mozart, and it has far too many notes." Wolfgang answered, quite confidently, "Just exactly as many notes as are needed, Your Majesty."

Mozart was a prolific composer, even at the age of six. His father notated the pieces Wolfgang wrote, in a notebook, recording the exact date of almost every composition. This minuet is dated January, 1762.

MINUET IN F MAJOR

This piece, unusual in its shifting phrases and rhythms, is probably the most remarkable of the compositions written by Mozart in his very early childhood. Mozart's sister, Nannerl, testified that this was written by Wolfgang when he was only five years old.

MINUET AND TRIO

in G Major

MINUET

Andante con moto

* Played: 

TRIO
f
p
mf
p
D. C. minuet al Fine

This minuet is dated July 5, 1762, and is the most advanced of three very similar minuets. It probably represents Wolfgang's third re-working of one composition, with the guidance of his first teacher, his father, Leopold Mozart.

MINUET IN F MAJOR

This well-known composition was originally a movement of a *divertimento* for wind instruments. The version below, published before 1800, is believed to be Mozart's own keyboard setting.

ANDANTE IN C MAJOR

dim.
f
p
sf
CODA
p
f

This is the first of eight minuets which Mozart composed in Salzburg in 1779, when he was 23 years old.

MINUET IN C MAJOR

* Played: 

** Play the small notes very rapidly, and *on the beat.*

Trio
legato
legato
più f
Minuet da capo
* Played:

A *contradance* consists of a series of 8-measure phrases which may be repeated as many times as desired. The name seems to have developed from the English *country dance,* which it resembles. Because it is often danced by two couples facing each other, the word *contra* ("against") has sometimes been associated with that aspect of the dance. This is one of several *contradances* Mozart composed in 1776 for Count Czernin, in exchange for one year's rent.

CONTRADANCE

in G Major

* Begin the trills on the upper note.

p
f
p
f
tr
f

Mozart's opera, *Don Giovanni,* is believed by many to be the greatest opera ever composed. It was a great success from its first performance in Prague, in October of 1787. The two most popular melodies from this opera are this famous *Minuet* and the vocal duet, *Là ci darem la mano* (page 16).

MINUET

from Don Giovanni

mf
legato
f
Fine
D. S. al Fine

This beautiful composition is one of the most charming of Mozart's works. It is sung by the heroine, Zerlina and Don Giovanni in the third scene of the first act of the opera. At the first performance of the opera the audience was so captivated by this duet that it had to be repeated three times. The title, in English, is usually given as *Give Me Your Hand, Zerlina.*

DUET FROM DON GIOVANNI

Lã ci darem la mano

cresc.
ritard.
a tempo
poco rit.

Mozart's opera, *The Marriage of Figaro,* was first performed in 1786. One of the singers in that first performance described the first rehearsal of the famous baritone aria, "Non più andrai": *I was standing close to Mozart, who stood on stage, dressed in a crimson coat and a gold-laced cocked hat, giving the beat to the orchestra. The singer, Benucci, sang with great animation and power, and I heard Mozart saying softly, "Bravo, Bravo, Benucci!" The effect of the piece was electrifying itself, for all of the performers and the whole orchestra, actuated by feelings of delight, shouted "Bravo! Bravo! Viva! Viva grande Mozart!" I thought they would never stop applauding!*

ARIA FROM "THE MARRIAGE OF FIGARO"

Non Più Andrai

1.
mf
2.
ff
ff

These two minuets are from Mozart's fourth keyboard sonata, composed in Salzburg in 1774. They are among his most popular keyboard compositions.

SONATA No. 4

MINUET I

Fine

MINUET II

D. C. Minuet I
al Fine

This piece was composed for glass harmonica, an unusual instrument invented by Benjamin Franklin in 1757. The tone was produced in the same manner as when a finger is rubbed on the rim of a wet glass. The instrument had a series of glasses of graduated sizes nestled one inside the other and rotating on a spindle. The glasses were made wet by turning in a trough of water. The instrument was played by touching the glasses as they revolved. Mozart himself played on such an instrument when he was 17. Because the glass harmonica is so very rare, this work is generally heard on the piano.

ADAGIO IN C MAJOR

for Glass Harmonica

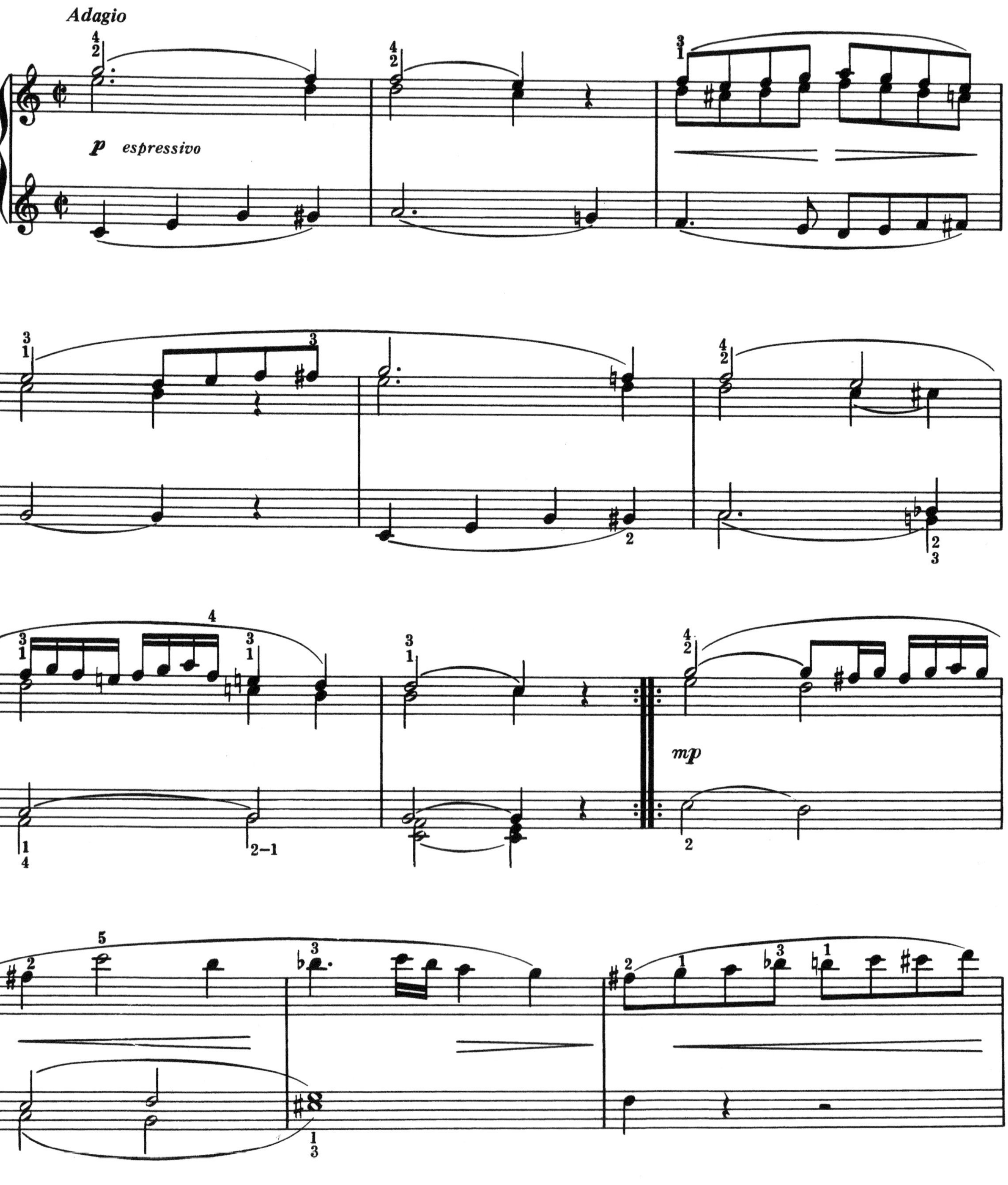

f
dim.
mf
mp
p

This *Allegretto* originates from a three-movement *Trio for Piano, Violin and Cello,* composed in October of 1788. The following setting for keyboard is believed to be Mozart's own version for piano alone.

ALLEGRETTO IN G MAJOR

Fine

dim.

p
rallentando
D. C. al Fine

Mozart's famous *Haffner Serenade,* composed in 1776, was originally scored for a small orchestra. The following keyboard version was first published in 1800, and is believed to be Mozart's own setting, for piano alone, for the 6th movement.

ANDANTE

from the Haffner Serenade

f
p
f
p
f
mf
p